P9-CQD-258

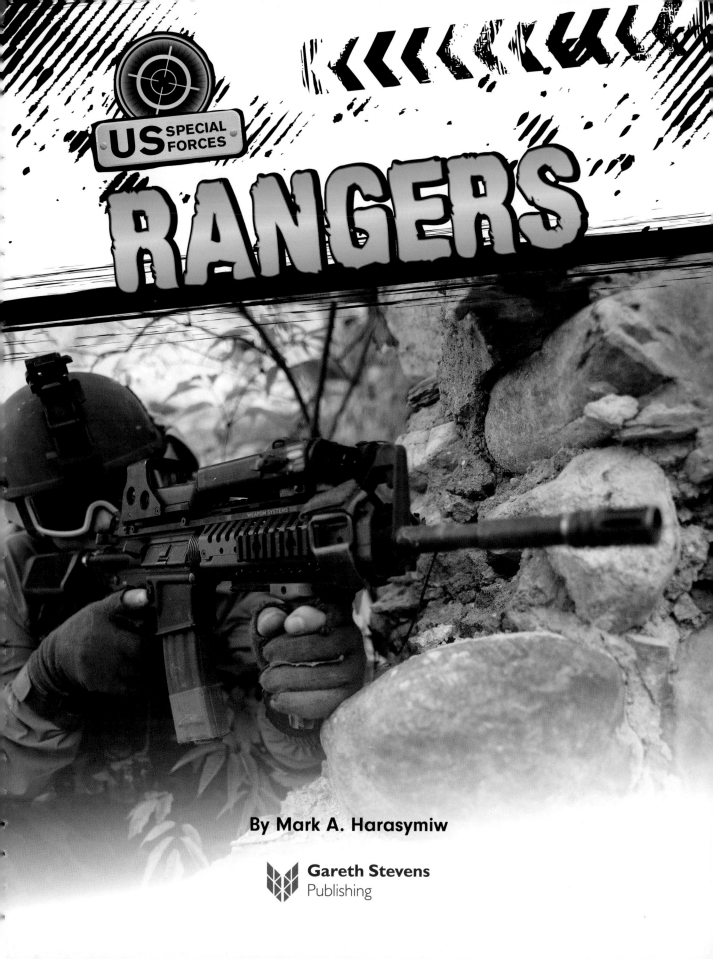

US SPECIAL FORCES

RANGERS

By Mark A. Harasymiw

Gareth Stevens
Publishing

Please visit our website, www.garethstevens.com. For a free color catalog of all our high-quality books, call toll free 1-800-542-2595 or fax 1-877-542-2596.

Library of Congress Cataloging-in-Publication Data

Harasymiw, Mark.
Rangers / Mark A. Harasymiw.
    p. cm. — (US Special Forces)
Includes index.
ISBN 978-1-4339-6575-3 (pbk.)
ISBN 978-1-4339-6576-0 (6-pack)
ISBN 978-1-4339-6573-9 (library binding)
1. United States. Army—Commando troops—Juvenile literature. I. Title.
UA34.R36H37 2011
356'.1670973—dc23

                                2011037099

First Edition

Published in 2012 by
Gareth Stevens Publishing
111 East 14th Street, Suite 349
New York, NY 10003

Copyright © 2012 Gareth Stevens Publishing

Designer: Michael J. Flynn
Editor: Kristen Rajczak

Photo credits: Cover, p. 1 MILpictures by Tom Weber/The Image Bank/Getty Images; photos courtesy of US Army: pp. 4–5 by US Army Center for Military History, 14, 19 by Jessica Bruckert USASOC Public Affairs, 15 by Capt. Manuel Menedez, 75th Army Rangers, 16–17 Patrick Albright, 18 by Sgt. Christopher M. Gaylord, 5th Mobile Public Affairs Detachment, 20 by SPC Zachary Gardner, 21 by John D. Helms, 23 by Staff Sgt. Michael J. Pryor (82nd Airborne), 24 by Ed Barker, 25 by Maj. Kamil Sztalkoper, 26–27 by 1st Platoon, B Company, 275th Ranger Regiment, 28–29 by USASOC; pp. 6, 9 MPI/Archive Photos/Getty Images; p. 7 Kean Collection/Archive Photos/Getty Images; p. 8 Three Lions/Hulton Archive/Getty Images; pp. 10–11 American Stock Archive/Archive Photos/Getty Images; p. 12 Keystone-France/Gamma-Keystone/Getty Images; p. 13 Bernard Hoffman/Time & Life Pictures/Getty Images.

Printed in the United States of America

CPSIA compliance information: Batch #CW12GS: For further information contact Gareth Stevens, New York, New York at 1-800-542-2595.

CONTENTS

Words in the glossary appear in **bold** type the first time they are used in the text.

INTRODUCING THE ARMY RANGERS

The US Army Rangers have a saying: "Rangers Lead the Way!" This saying comes from one of the most important events in US Army history—D-Day.

This illustration shows US troops fighting their way into France on D-Day.

On June 6, 1944, **Allied** troops **invaded** France to free it from German forces. During this battle on a beach in Normandy, the troops' **mission** was to climb the nearby cliffs and fight the German army positioned there. An American general, realizing the ascent was going to be difficult, is believed to have said to a group of Army Rangers, "Rangers, lead the way!"

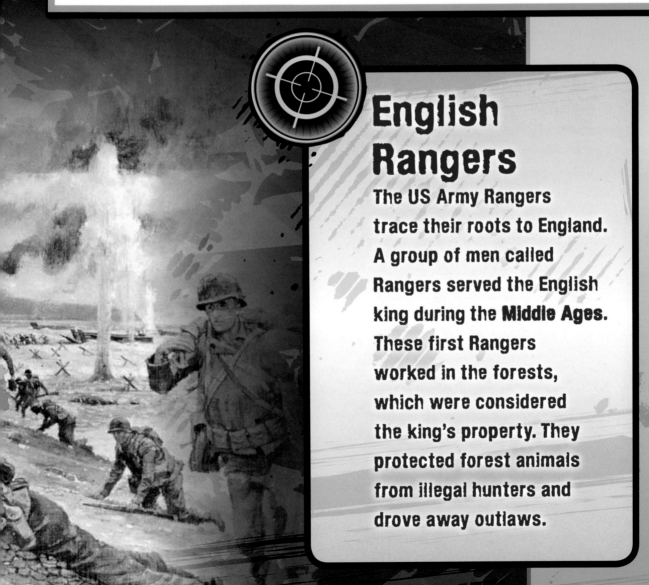

English Rangers

The US Army Rangers trace their roots to England. A group of men called Rangers served the English king during the **Middle Ages.** These first Rangers worked in the forests, which were considered the king's property. They protected forest animals from illegal hunters and drove away outlaws.

RANGER ROOTS

The first American Rangers organized soon after the British colonies were settled in North America. In the 1600s and 1700s, Native Americans populated much of the land the colonists lived on. Some Native Americans were friendly to British colonists, and some were not.

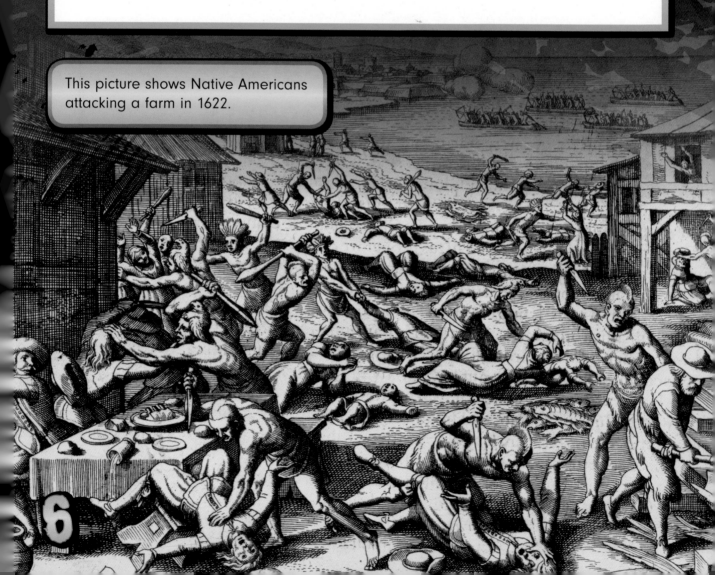

This picture shows Native Americans attacking a farm in 1622.

The Native Americans didn't fight like other enemies the [Brit]ish knew. They attacked swiftly and then scattered. British [col]onists needed a new type of soldier to stop Native American [rai]ds. These soldiers needed to know how to survive in the [un]explored areas of the wild and be tough and fast.

Soldiers in the Wild

King Philip

Captain Benjamin Church organized the first group of American Rangers in 1670. These men used the Native Americans' fighting style to find and kill a Wampanoag chief they called King Philip. They spent long periods of time "ranging," or quietly searching, for him. This is how modern Rangers got their name.

Major Robert Rogers and his Rangers are shown in this illustration from 1758.

During the mid-1700s, the British army formed groups of Rangers to protect the colonies during England's war with France. These Rangers helped the British attack the French and their Native American allies.

One of the earliest Ranger groups was called "Rogers's Rangers" after its leader, Major Robert Rogers. He led his men through hundreds of miles of wilderness to raid a Native American village in Quebec, Canada. The ability to attack deep inside enemy territory without being discovered was as valuable to these early Rangers as it is to today's US Army Rangers.

Revolutionary Rangers

Ranger units also formed to help the Continental army fight the British during the **American Revolution**. A man named Dan Morgan commanded these Rangers. Francis Marion, a military officer also known as the "Swamp Fox," led a group of Rangers, too. They were called "Marion's **Partisans**."

Francis Marion is shown leading his troops during the American Revolution in this picture.

The American Civil War was a conflict between the Northern and Southern states that took place from 1861 to 1865. During this time, Ranger units carried out missions for both sides. One of the most famous **Confederate** Ranger units was Mosby's Rangers.

Led by John Singleton Mosby, Mosby's Rangers had success raiding deep behind **Union** lines, passing thousands of soldiers unnoticed. In 1863, Mosby's Rangers tried to capture an officer from his headquarters in Virginia. Although they didn't find the man they wanted, they were able to capture a general, many soldiers, and a large number of horses.

Morgan's Rangers

Besides making raids deep into enemy territory to capture soldiers, Rangers also worked to cut off supply lines. One unit, led by General John Hunt Morgan, snuck by Northern forces to blow up train tracks. This made it difficult for the Union army to supply its troops with food and other materials needed to fight the war.

Morgan's Rangers are shown attacking a village during the Civil War in this picture.

WORLD WAR II RANGERS

The next major war that US Army Rangers fought in was World War II. Their units were made up of US Army **volunteers**. Their training was based on that of British **Commandos**. The specially skilled commandos had been fighting in the war since it began. Their experiences with the German army were used in training the new American Rangers.

British Commandos and US Army Rangers both train to move quietly behind enemy lines.

In addition to "leading the way" in France on D-Day in 1944, the Rangers helped invade North Africa in 1942 and Italy in 1943. They also fought in Asia against the Japanese. This tradition of fighting in many different areas of the world is shared by the Rangers of today.

The men pictured here were members of the 5307th Composite Unit—Merrill's Marauders.

Merrill's Marauders

Merrill's Marauders were a group of US Army Rangers who fought in Southeast Asia during World War II. Named for their leader Frank Merrill, the Marauders' mission was to cut off Japanese communications and supply lines. They walked more than 1,000 miles (1,609 km) while successfully battling Japanese forces in the jungle.

MODERN RANGERS

During the **Vietnam War**, the US Army needed a group of soldiers for long-range patrols. These soldiers would have to stay behind enemy lines for long periods of time, discover enemy positions, and complete **reconnaissance** missions.

At first, these long-range patrol units weren't called Rangers. However, their missions and abilities were very much like the Ranger units from earlier wars, such as Mosby's Rangers and Merrill's Marauders. These long-range patrol units eventually became part of Ranger units already fighting in Vietnam. The army officially created the 1st Ranger Battalion of the 75th Ranger Regiment in 1974.

Rangers from the 75th Ranger Regiment take part in a training raid in 2011.

Rangers move an injured soldier during an international military competition.

Constant Rangers

Before the 1970s, US Army Ranger units were disbanded, or shut down, after each war ended. During the Vietnam War, Ranger units were formed to take on the many difficult missions that needed a special group of soldiers. Afterwards, some units weren't disbanded, paving the way for the units of today.

THE 75TH REGIMENT

Today's US Army Rangers are organized into a single unit, the 75th Ranger Regiment. The 75th Ranger Regiment is made up of four units called battalions. Each battalion is made up of no more than 580 soldiers, including riflemen and support staff.

Rangers from the 3rd Battalion train for a raid.

US Army Rangers have missions that require them to be able to operate both day and night, during any type of weather, and on any kind of **terrain**. Rangers are trained to capture enemies and enemy-held territory. They know how to do these missions quickly, quietly, and effectively. Rangers are also trained for reconnaissance.

The Fourth Battalion

The newest battalion in the 75th Ranger Regiment formed in 2006. The Rangers Special Troops Battalion, or RSTB, helps the first three Ranger battalions as well as other military units. It gives communications and reconnaissance support. The RSTB also finds and trains soldiers who want to become Rangers.

RANGER TRAINING

There are three phases, or stages, of training that most **recruits** must go through to join the 75th Ranger Regiment. However, before this training, each recruit must first complete the Ranger Assessment and Selection Program, or RASP.

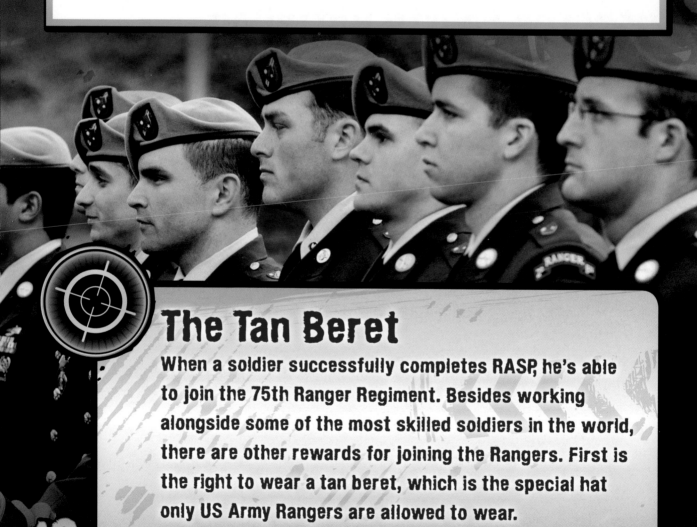

The Tan Beret

When a soldier successfully completes RASP, he's able to join the 75th Ranger Regiment. Besides working alongside some of the most skilled soldiers in the world, there are other rewards for joining the Rangers. First is the right to wear a tan beret, which is the special hat only US Army Rangers are allowed to wear.

RASP not only teaches the basic skills necessary to be a Ranger but also makes certain the recruit has the physical and mental toughness needed to be a US Army Ranger. All recruits must pass Airborne School. This includes, most importantly, successfully parachuting from an airplane. Rangers are also taught and tested on first aid and advanced life-saving procedures.

Rangers use their parachute training to sneak behind enemy lines.

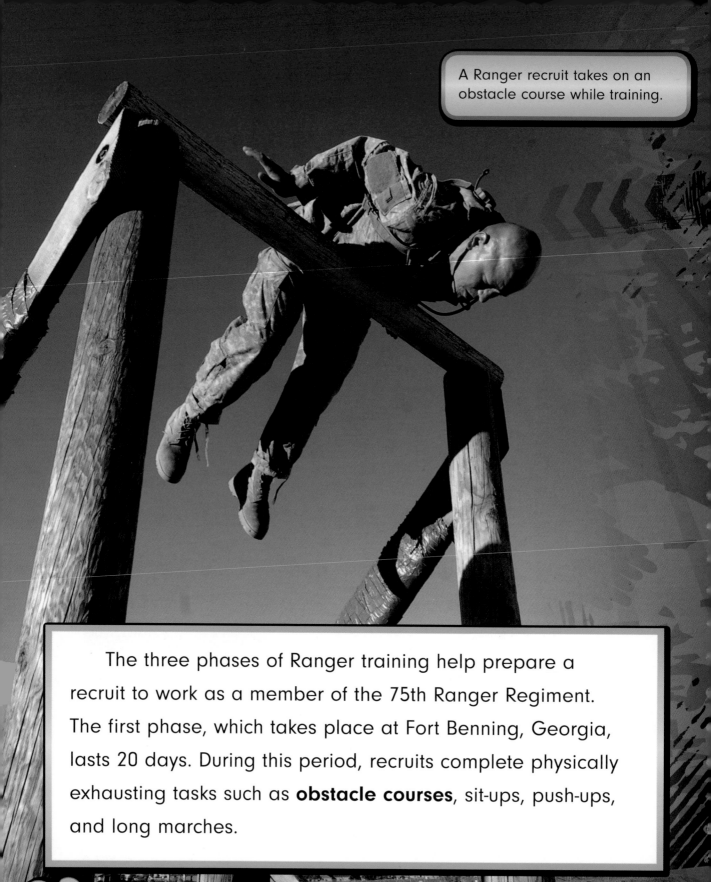

A Ranger recruit takes on an obstacle course while training.

The three phases of Ranger training help prepare a recruit to work as a member of the 75th Ranger Regiment. The first phase, which takes place at Fort Benning, Georgia, lasts 20 days. During this period, recruits complete physically exhausting tasks such as **obstacle courses**, sit-ups, push-ups, and long marches.

The second phase is the 20-day mountain phase. During this time, recruits must work together in small groups in rugged mountain terrain while getting little sleep and eating little.

The final stage takes place in Florida and lasts 16 days. This phase teaches recruits how to operate in swamps and jungles as well as exercise leadership skills.

Rangers need to be able to work in all kinds of conditions.

Toughening Up

Between physical training, sleeping outside, and eating less than normal, recruits can lose 20 to 30 pounds (9 to 14 kg) by the end of the three phases of training. As hard as training is, it teaches recruits valuable lessons and proves they're tough enough to be US Army Rangers.

GETTING THERE

Rangers perform missions all over the world in many kinds of terrain. Each mission has to be approached differently. Rangers reach the area where they will perform their mission in different ways, depending on where it will take place. They may parachute from airplanes. Rangers also use small rubber boats to travel to locations.

Another common way to travel to a mission start area is by helicopter. Rangers slide down to the ground using a special rope. However, once the Rangers reach their start location, they march to complete their mission. From training and exercise, Rangers have a lot of practice marching.

Always Ready

The Rangers have a system that makes certain at least one battalion is ready to go anywhere in the world within 18 hours. For 13 weeks, one Ranger battalion is ready with all weapons and supplies necessary for a mission. After that 13-week period, it's the next battalion's turn to be ready.

Some helicopters
transport more
than just troops!

23

WEAPONS

The Army Rangers often perform missions on foot after they reach a certain area. This allows them to continue moving in secret. They must carry all their gear with them. Most Rangers carry a lightweight but powerful rifle called an M4A1 Carbine. Some carry machine guns for times when extra firepower is needed.

The Army Rangers bring men trained as snipers on missions. These soldiers are able to shoot very well from a great distance without being noticed by the enemy. The snipers use a special rifle that can hit targets more than a mile (1.6 km) away.

A Ranger fires his M4.

24

Special Weapons

When the Rangers need to hit targets too large or well armored for the M4A1, they have more powerful weapons they can use. Against targets on the ground, they use the Ranger Antitank Weapons System, or RAWS. The RAWS can fire many rounds at a time. It's sometimes called a Carl Gustav, after its inventor.

MODERN WARFARE

Today's US Army Rangers have been on the front lines of many modern conflicts involving the United States. In 1993, a unit of Rangers was in Somalia as part of a military force working to bring peace to the country.

In October 1993, the Rangers undertook a mission to capture several Somali warlords. During the mission, the warlords' soldiers shot down two US helicopters, killing several Rangers. More Rangers were sent in to rescue the survivors. For nearly 18 hours, they fought Somali soldiers. About 600 Somali soldiers died while only six Rangers were lost.

Recent Missions

More recently, the Rangers have fought in Iraq and Afghanistan. In October 2001, the 3rd Battalion successfully conducted an airborne assault to seize an airfield as part of Operation Enduring Freedom in Afghanistan. March 2003 found the 3rd Battalion leading the way by completing the first airborne assault during Operation Iraqi Freedom.

The Rangers photographed here were stationed in Afghanistan in 2003.

THE FUTURE OF THE RANGERS

When the Ranger battalions were established in 1974, General Creighton Abrams, Army Chief of Staff, said he wanted the Rangers to be the best of the army and a model for the rest of the army. Besides being physically strong, Rangers would be smart, tough, and courageous.

Abrams believed every Ranger unit would be excellent because each individual Ranger would be highly skilled and have great character. It's these qualities, combined with the lessons learned throughout US Army Rangers' history, that will serve the Rangers well in future conflicts.

A Ranger watches for the enemy while on duty in Iraq.

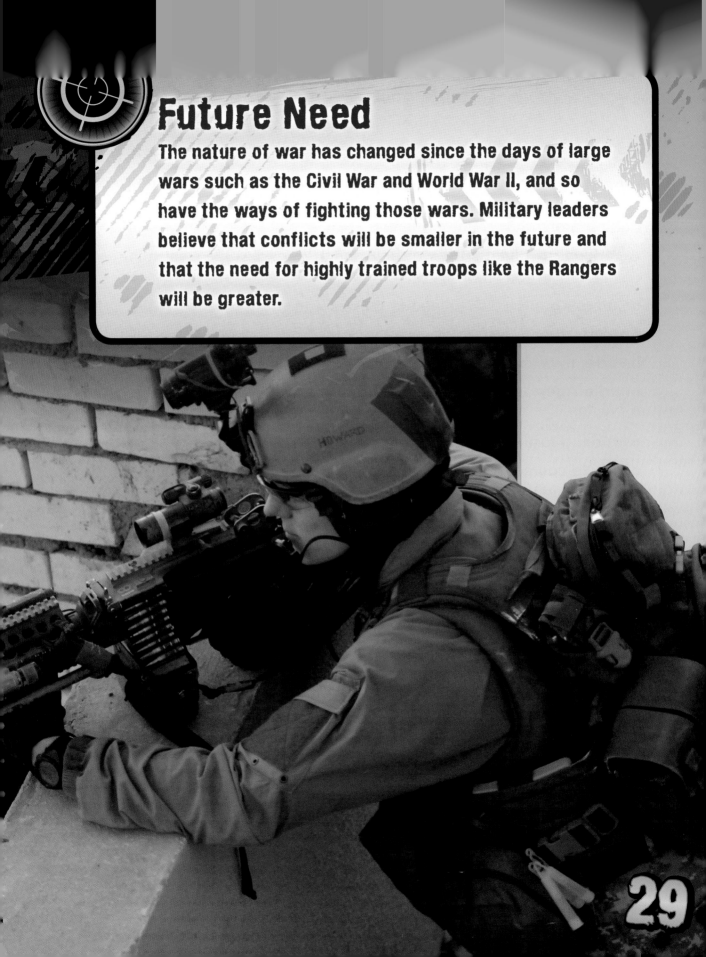

Future Need

The nature of war has changed since the days of large wars such as the Civil War and World War II, and so have the ways of fighting those wars. Military leaders believe that conflicts will be smaller in the future and that the need for highly trained troops like the Rangers will be greater.

GLOSSARY

Allied: having to do with the group of countries that included the United States during World War II. An ally is a person or country with which another person or country is united.

American Revolution: the war between 1775 and 1783 in which the colonists overthrew British control

commando: a soldier trained to make surprise attacks

Confederate: having to do with the Southern states during the Civil War

invade: to enter by force

Middle Ages: the period of European history between the years 500 and 1500

mission: a task or job a group must perform

obstacle course: a training area in which objects such as fences and ditches have to be climbed or crossed over

partisan: a soldier who fights in enemy territory

reconnaissance: the exploration of a place to collect information

recruit: a new member of a military force

terrain: the features of a piece of land

Union: having to do with the Northern states during the Civil War

Vietnam War: a conflict starting in 1955 and ending in 1975 between South Vietnam and North Vietnam in which the United States joined with South Vietnam

volunteer: a person who offers to do something

FOR MORE INFORMATION

Books

Alvarez, Carlos. *Army Rangers*. Minneapolis, MN: Bellwether Media, 2010.

Braulick, Carrie A. *The U.S. Army Rangers*. Mankato, MN: Blazers, 2006.

Sandler, Michael. *Army Rangers in Action*. New York, NY: Bearport Publishing, 2008.

Websites

How the Army Rangers Work
science.howstuffworks.com/army-Ranger.htm
Learn more about Ranger training and operations.

US Army: 75th Ranger Regiment
www.goarmy.com/ranger.html
Read about the Rangers on the official US Army website.

Publisher's note to educators and parents: Our editors have carefully reviewed these websites to ensure that they are suitable for students. Many websites change frequently, however, and we cannot guarantee that a site's future contents will continue to meet our high standards of quality and educational value. Be advised that students should be closely supervised whenever they access the Internet.

INDEX